FROM THE LOVING-KINDNESS MONK

Morning Coffee with Bhante

A Collection of Inspirational Wisdom from Venerable Bhante Sujatha & Noble Friends

All rights reserved
Cover page image by Chamila Wijethunga
Cover design by Jessica Dunegan
Interior layout and design by Britta Fithian-Zurn
First Edition 2020
ISBN 978-1-7327758-2-4 paperback
ISBN 978-1-7327758-3-1 hardcover
ISBN 978-1-7327758-4-8 eBook

Morning Coffee with Bhante

CONTENTS

Foreword
Introduction
Dedication

Impermanence & Non-Attachment
Peace & Loving-Kindness
I, Me, My, Mine & Ego
Meditation & Mindfulness
The Nature of Nature
Overcoming Obstacles
Anger & Hatred
Take the Time
Silent Observation
Rethinking Relationships

FOREWORD

Sometimes the deepest truths are not found through the development of long scholarly arguments backed up by logic and reference. Sometimes they are already within us, waiting in the background to be recognized. Waiting to penetrate our consciousness in a moment of true openness.

Lessons like these often come in a few simple words. Leaving us saying, "Yes! That's what I was thinking!"

In this collection, Bhante Sujatha shares with us this kind of wisdom: easy to remember, fun, practical, deep, and subtle. The words resonate with us, because they illuminate truths of the life we all share. As Bhante says, "we are all brothers and sisters, one large family."

Bhante often says that these thoughts don't belong to him. They come from within; but are a result of the hard work of a lifetime of mindfulness training. He shares these fruits of his practice each day with thousands of people around the globe. Every day, at least one person feels that Bhante is speaking directly to them, telling them exactly what they needed to hear.

As you move through this small collection again and again, you will discover something new with each reading. You will find these lessons developing within. Until one day you will read something that was exactly what you needed to hear, at exactly the right time. And it will change your life forever.

MICHAEL FRONCZAK – Moderator of "Morning Coffee with Bhante"
& Co-Founder of Sanatha Suwaya

INTRODUCTION

People always ask me, "Bhante, how are you feeling?" I've struggled how to answer because my heart and mind are separate from my body. We all have an imperfect body and so often the answer is that I don't feel good. But I have no expectation to feel good all the time. I simply want to feel mindful and compassionate. My mindfulness practice is what makes me feel good in any particular moment, not how my body feels. So, today my answer is, "I am feeling really good! I am happy, peaceful and well."

It is my hope that this book will serve to guide you as much as my daily morning coffee messages have over the years. When you need an inspirational message, thought, or mantra for your practice, turn to a random page or a specific chapter for encouragement.

Be well, happy and peaceful,
Bhante Sujatha

DEDICATION

For all the mothers.
The love they have within radiates outward…
touching lives with the power to change the world.

IMPERMANENCE
&
NON-ATTACHMENT

Everything is connected.
Be a strong and beautiful link in the chain of life,
until you are ready to let go completely.

Impermanence & Non-Attachment

Letting go is the
hardest thing to do,
but remains the
best option for solving
our personal problems.

Impermanence & Non-Attachment

It is okay to have expectations, but they must be handled with care. The best preparation for managing them, is to develop our minds to accept and understand the nature of impermanence in life.

Impermanence & Non-Attachment

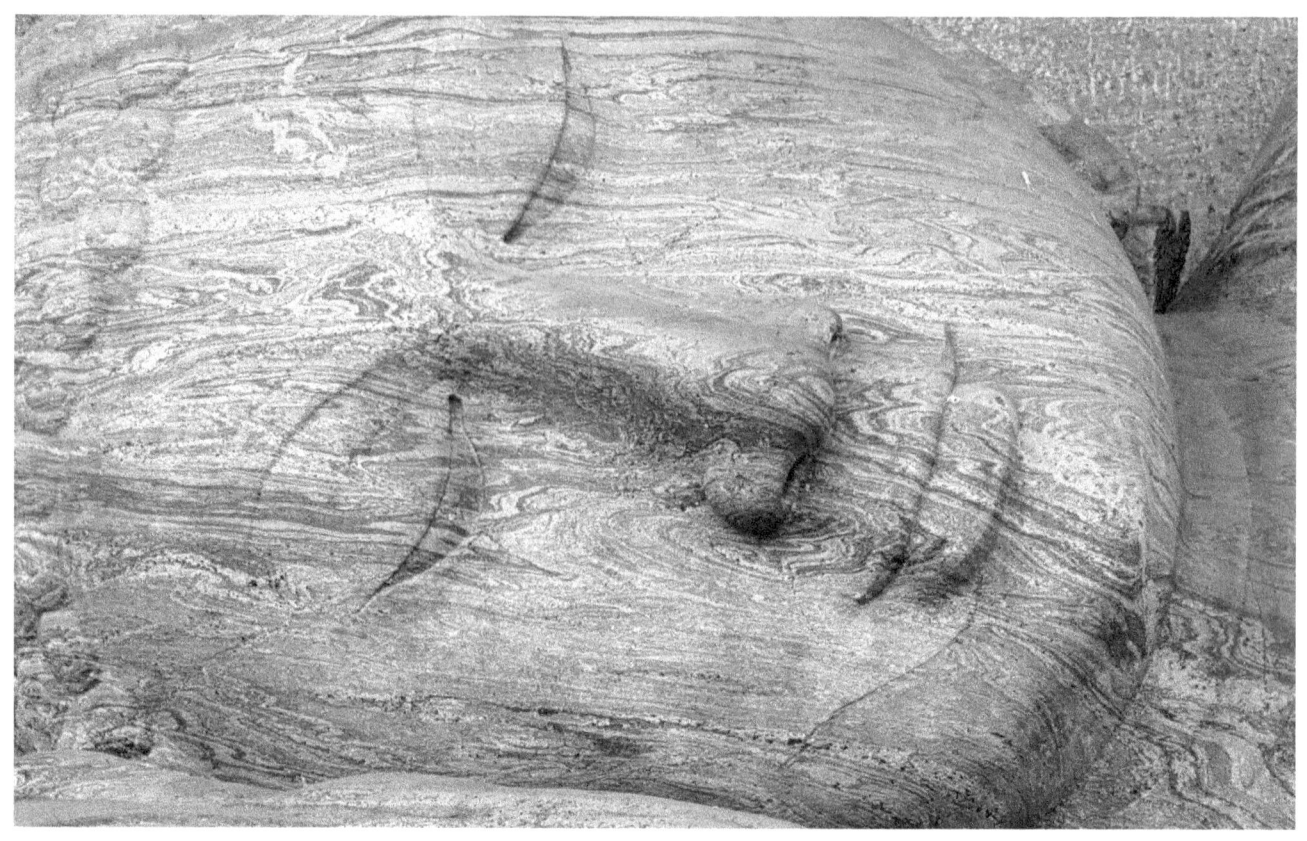

A task for you: Make a commitment to bringing
your full attention to one moment today.
Write a note about it to yourself. Read the note
tomorrow morning. Reflect on it. Then let it go.

Impermanence & Non-Attachment

We do not let go
of the world,
we let go of
attachment itself.

Impermanence & Non-Attachment

Don't keep so many expectations about people.
Even those who promise their life to you,
can change their mind in a moment.

Impermanence & Non-Attachment

If you truly understand
impermanence, you can
see the path to happiness.

Impermanence & Non-Attachment

Without a self to possess them,
what lasting value could be found in possessions?

Impermanence & Non-Attachment

Nothing endures
but change.

Impermanence & Non-Attachment

Rather than a problem to be solved,
impermanence is a fundamental
characteristic of existence.

Impermanence & Non-Attachment

Thoughts and attachments are like clouds that pass.
Let them move on naturally to see your way clearly.

Impermanence & Non-Attachment

Peace & Loving-Kindness

All living creatures are beautiful;
all beings are worthy of loving-kindness.

Peace & Loving-Kindness

Compassion and loving-kindness are not weaknesses.
They require great patience, courage and endurance.
They are not passive, but active:
When events come to our lives, we must take action
that is guided by mindfulness, not emotion.

Peace & Loving-Kindness

When you put on shoes, think;
there are many who go without shoes,
when you drink water, think;
there are many who go without water.
Practicing in this way, loving-kindness will develop
in your mind and lead to action.

Peace & Loving-Kindness

Compassion
is rooted in love,
refined by practice
and established
through action.

Peace & Loving-Kindness

There are a handful of people who can dry tears with a smile. Their hearts are open and they always have room for one more person in their lives.

Peace & Loving-Kindness

All beings seek comfort;
be an agent of peace
for the world.

Peace & Loving-Kindness

Those who have not received love from the world,
and still give love to the world, are those
who truly understand its value.

Peace & Loving-Kindness

A person's most useful asset is not a head full of knowledge but a heart full of love with ears ready to listen and a willing heart to help others.

Peace & Loving-Kindness

Loving-kindness
is a universal language
that everyone can speak.

Peace & Loving-Kindness

7 Guidelines For Adding Happiness To Life

Avoid letting thoughts develop into anger

Don't worry about what is lost

Live simply

Give more

Have less expectation

Smile often

Develop and maintain a daily loving-kindness practice

Peace & Loving-Kindness

I, Me, My, Mine & Ego

You don't have to be perfect, to love yourself.

I, Me, My, Mine & Ego

When you are poor, be honest.
When you are rich, be simple.
When you have power, exercise discipline.
When you are angry, be silent.

I, Me, My, Mine & Ego

The only true and lasting capital that a successful person possesses is a strong and courageous mind.

I, Me, My, Mine & Ego

Understand that the "self"
is a process, not a thing.

I, Me, My, Mine & Ego

Love yourself
and others will follow.

I, Me, My, Mine & Ego

You have the power to heal yourself.
It begins by holding yourself
with love and acceptance.

I, Me, My, Mine & Ego

You are what you are looking for.

I, Me, My, Mine & Ego

The world is too big for you to change
but you are big enough to change yourself.

I, Me, My, Mine & Ego

Pride is a link in the bonds of attachment.
For the egotistical person, one day it will be all
that remains. To study your ego, practice humility,
and watch yourself closely.

I, Me, My, Mine & Ego

We look in the mirror everyday but we still can't
find ourselves. Looking in the mirror is not enough,
we have to understand mindfully what we see.

I, Me, My, Mine & Ego

Meditation & Mindfulness

Words can cut as deep as the sharpest blade,
heal as ably as the most soothing balm,
and can cross great lengths of time.
Therefore, listen with your ears and your heart
guided by mindful attention.

Meditation & Mindfulness

A part of mindfulness is selective thinking,
which is choosing the thoughts we focus on, instead
of connecting with whatever thought enters our mind.

Meditation & Mindfulness

Compassion, generosity, and gratitude, are virtues that must be cultivated through mindfulness practice. Develop yourself and you immediately benefit others.

Meditation & Mindfulness

Help yourself. Help others.
Realize that you cannot help everyone or fix everything. Doing your best and accepting reality will allow you to support others mindfully.

Meditation & Mindfulness

Sometimes challenges come at us with more strength
and speed than we think that we can handle.
The truth is, challenges are always coming at us, but some
are just easier to see than others. Mindfulness practice
teaches us both how to see, and how to handle all of them.

Meditation & Mindfulness

Like the waves and the wind, our minds
are always moving. Don't try to control their flow,
just observe their movements and enjoy.

Meditation & Mindfulness

Make your breath
the starting point
of every journey.

Meditation & Mindfulness

Living does not mean
just maintaining life,
but using all of our senses
to live mindfully.

Meditation & Mindfulness

There is a path.
We have to walk it ourself.
Find your way
and take each step
with awareness.

Meditation & Mindfulness

When you practice
introspective awareness,
regrets transform
into lessons.

Meditation & Mindfulness

The Nature of Nature

The most beautiful flower
can rise from even
the murkiest of waters.

The Nature of Nature

Allow nature to inspire you to meditate.

The Nature of Nature

In difficult times when the path is hard to see,
remember well that it hasn't vanished,
but that our view has changed.

The Nature of Nature

Consider your mind as a sacred garden.
Tend to it daily, cultivate it carefully,
and watch it grow into something beautiful.

When you feel stuck in one place,
stop trying to get somewhere. For just a moment,
simply look around at where you are.
The view may surprise you.

The Nature of Nature

Your good deeds are like the seeds of a beautiful flower. Nurture, and allow them to grow. Don't hurry to harvest them for yourself. They will bloom in their own time, and be enjoyed by many.

The Nature of Nature

In a moment of crisis, it is easy to feel overwhelmed. Observe the vast and changing nature of life to reflect carefully before you react.

The Nature of Nature

When you like a flower,
you simply pluck it.
When you love a flower,
you water it daily.

The Nature of Nature

Even in our modern lives we can still learn
and practice to work in harmony with the earth.
Strive to give more than you take,
and leave behind something beautiful.

The Nature of Nature

When the rain falls, you have no choice but to let it fall.
Be still, and watch the rain come and go.

The Nature of Nature

Overcoming Obstacles

You are both the problem and the solution.

Overcoming Obstacles

Reflect on how much
energy you have spent
on fear and worry.

Overcoming Obstacles

Don't base your beliefs on another's account
of what is good or bad. In short, don't build your life
around the opinions of others; listen, think,
and decide who you want to be.

Overcoming Obstacles

Try patience when it absolutely seems like you can't
go even an inch further. Just wait a moment.
Then decide if you want to give up or keep going.

Overcoming Obstacles

Good days bring pleasure. Bad days bring experience.
Both are important. Enjoy the good days, and appreciate
the bad ones. Keep the courage it takes to live life fully.

Overcoming Obstacles

When you experience suffering in your mind,
don't search for the responsible person or situation.
Use your energy to understand the root of your
suffering and allow yourself to release it.

Overcoming Obstacles

If we take the negative emotions from our past into our future, we will miss our happiness.

Overcoming Obstacles

Look carefully at the weight you carry and understand how it is your choice whether to put it down or not.

Overcoming Obstacles

Practice acceptance when facing challenges
that life presents you with. Learning to solve
problems, and how to prevent them in the future,
comes through acceptance and patience:
not by struggle and despair.

Overcoming Obstacles

We all have problems, no matter who we are.
Having problems and managing problems
are two different things.

Overcoming Obstacles

Anger & Hatred

Tolerance does not mean letting others harm you.
It means learning to stop hurting yourself by
understanding and addressing what is truly injurious,
and releasing what is inconsequential.

Anger & Hatred

When somebody hurts you, don't respond with anger.
Instead, practice loving-kindness towards them.
This is an effective way to study and
teach the lesson of pain and suffering.

Anger & Hatred

Difficult people are a part of life. They give us the
opportunity to see ourselves. Think of them
as your teachers and friends, and if you feel anger,
understand that you are only harming yourself.

Anger & Hatred

One of life's
greatest offerings
is the opportunity
to overcome anger.

Hasty words that
are spoken in anger,
create walls that are
not easily broken.

Anger & Hatred

You will not be punished for your anger. You will be punished by anger.

Anger & Hatred

Anger and hatred inspire the urge to break.
Compassion and love inspire the urge to build.

Anger & Hatred

Anger is a force that can consume you until you are so enveloped that you can no longer remember why you first became angry.

Anger & Hatred

Let go: not through anger or fear, but through understanding.

Anger & Hatred

Take the Time

In times of frustration and doubt,
reflecting on gratitude is a good guide
to return us back to our mindfulness practice.

Take the Time

Knowledge is learning through another's experience.
Wisdom comes from learning through your own.

Take the Time

Don't try to measure your progress.
Every path is taken one step at a time.
You'll know when you have arrived.

Take the Time

Life keeps going. Trying to stop or hold it
only leads to disappointment. Learn to move
with life, and find peace within.

Take the Time

Don't wait.
Don't wait for the
right time, the right place,
or the right setting.
Life is not waiting for you;
it is simply ready
for your attention.

Take the Time

Patience is not how long you wait, but how you behave while you wait.

Take the Time

To live truly,
keep yourself in
the present moment.
Expectations live in
the future.

Take the Time

Death is a phase of life. Reflecting on it is not
a negative process, but a natural one. Be mindful
that one day we all must leave, and see it
help you to live your life fully.

Take the Time

No need to regret errors
you made in the past.
Just focus on the
opportunity to do good
in the present moment.

Take the Time

Can we guess how many more years
we are going live life in this world? Hurry up!
There is no time to waste. Time to enjoy life!
Live mindfully, die mindfully.

Take the Time

Silent Observation

The line where being alone becomes loneliness
is created according to our understanding of solitude.

Silent Observation

No matter how the world is moving, it is when
we are still and quiet that wisdom is revealed to us.

Silent Observation

Make time for solitude in your life. One who is given solitude can learn to know things as they truly are.

Silent Observation

Just be still and pay attention. That is all you have to do.

Silent Observation

Be silent, let go of time, and allow
the flowing mindfulness to reveal the wisdom
our busyness hides from us.

Silent Observation

Take time for solitude
and then use it wisely.

Silent Observation

If you only stare into the distance you are bound to miss a step in front of you.

Silent Observation

If you want
to understand reality,
please practice silence.

Silent Observation

Silence is everywhere you are; listen closely, and you will hear it.

Silent Observation

Wisdom is calling from within; silence yourself to hear it.

Silent Observation

Rethinking Relationships

Before racism disconnects us, before religion divides us, before politics separates us, let us remember that we are a human family.

Rethinking Relationships

Whoever comes to our life, will leave our life. Always.
We have something to learn from each experience.
Some are painful, some are not, but there is always
a lesson there to teach us something meaningful.

Rethinking Relationships

Among the many acquaintances we make, there will be Noble Friends. Look carefully for them and honor their companionship.

Rethinking Relationships

Many will speak of your weaknesses, but it is a true friend who will discuss them kindly and directly with you.

Rethinking Relationships

If you have only one companion in your life
whom you can trust without reservation, you have
found one of existence's greatest gifts.

Rethinking Relationships

There are many roads,
but they all share
the same earth.

Rethinking Relationships

We are far too prone to creating divisions between others and ourselves. We have to work to build bridges of union.

Rethinking Relationships

When someone hurts you, before trying to hurt them back, or deciding on how to react, consider that individual's situation in life. In this way, you develop wisdom, and protect yourself.

Rethinking Relationships

We have no way to know exactly where or when
we will encounter others throughout our journey.
Today's rival could be tomorrow's friend.

Rethinking Relationships

GRATITUDE

A feast for the eyes and a feast for the soul.
This beautiful book was truly a global project. Gratitude goes out to all who helped make this possible.

The Physical Creation of the Book

- Bhante Assiji – Designer & Buddhist Monk, Woodstock, Illinois & Peradeniya, Sri Lanka
- Britta Fithian-Zurn and Cora – Designer & Book Formatter, Portland, Oregon
- Diane Thompson Skidmore – Project Manager/Editor, Bloomington, Illinois
- Eric V. Van Der Hope – Book Publishing Strategist & Shepherd, Los Angeles, California
- Jessica Dunegan – Designer, Illustrator, Yogi & Cover Designer, Augusta, Kansas
- Katherine Tragasz – Designer, Greyslake, Illinois

This book could not have been possible without the expertise, professionalism, diligence and love of these individuals. Sadhu! Sadhu! Sadhu!

The Wisdom

- Venerable Bhante Sujatha – Woodstock, IL, Peradeniya, Sri Lanka & the World-at-Large
- Michael Fronczak – Moderator of "Morning Coffee with Bhante" Peradeniya, Sri Lanka
- All the contributors known and unknown. We send to them our humble appreciation for the wisdom that we have included in this book.

Powerful wisdom takes on a life of its own as it is shared from person to person. We acknowledge that the origins of several passages are unknown to us and make no claim that all originated from Bhante Sujatha, Michael or our Noble Friends. Our purpose is solely to end suffering and add more love to the world.

The Photographic Images

- Ann Mays – Artist, Poet & Photographer, Carbondale, Illinois
- Ben Sykora – Student, Philanthropist & Photographer, Boulder, Colorado & Hebron, Illinois
- Chamila Wijethunga – Graphic Designer & Photographer, Kandy, Sri Lanka
- Diane Thompson Skidmore – Artist & Monk's Personal Assistant, Bloomington, Illinois
- Doug Johnson – Artist & McLean County Art Center – Director, Normal, Illinois
- Evan Skidmore - Photographer, Bloomington, Illinois
- Jim and Kathy Simonik – Noble Friends, Sedona, Arizona
- Marsha Skidmore - Designer, Fennville, Michigan
- Michael Fronczak – Co-Founder of Sanatha Suwaya, Peradeniya, Sri Lanka & Roseville, Michigan
- Pam Holland – Artist & Photographer, Adelaide, South Australia
- Noble Friends who have shared their beautiful images with Bhante Sujatha over the years

A special "thank you" to each person who so generously shared their photographs with us. The images in this book reveal the astonishing beauty of our world. Their color, texture, and emotion give an extra dimension of wonder and contemplation to the wisdom in this book.

ABOUT BHANTE SUJATHA

Ordained as a Buddhist monk in his native Sri Lanka at the age of eleven, Venerable Bhante Sujatha is singularly focused on adding more love to the world. The founder and Spiritual Director of the Blue Lotus Temple and Meditation Center in Woodstock, IL, Bhante leads a regional congregation and teaches loving-kindness to people seeking the art of contentment worldwide.

Bhante gives more that 380 talks and guided meditations annually. He travels hundreds of thousands of miles, often going straight from the plane to a podium. Speaking at temples, churches, meditation centers, yoga studios, schools and universities; he teaches that love is the way and peace is a constant practice.

His annual humanitarian work spans the globe. Recent charitable projects include; bringing much needed supplies, construction and technology to under-funded Sri Lankan schools, creation of a tube well system to bring drinking water to a parched community, and support of pregnant mother's spiritual and medical needs—including donating incubators and ultrasound equipment to maternity hospitals in his home country.

In recognition of his invaluable impact in spreading Buddhism in America. Bhante was awarded the highest honor within his lineage when he was named the Chief Sangha Nayake of North America in 2013.

Bhante's approach to meditation is deep and simple. He shares core Buddhist teachings in ways that are practical and easy to understand. A radiant, funny, and wildly energetic monk, Bhante helps people attain peace that can only be found in deep silence.

www.bhantesujatha.org

www.ingramcontent.com/pod-product-compliance
Lightning Source LLC
Chambersburg PA
CBHW061126070526
44584CB00033B/4232